Original title:
Singularity Sonnets

Copyright © 2025 Creative Arts Management OÜ
All rights reserved.

Author: Milo Harrington
ISBN HARDBACK: 978-1-80567-849-6
ISBN PAPERBACK: 978-1-80567-970-7

The Convergence of Voices

In a world where all thoughts collide,
Cats and robots dance side by side.
A toaster chirps like a bird in flight,
While socks debate if black or white.

Fragments of Enigmatic Light

A light bulb flickers with secret glee,
It whispers tales from the deep blue sea.
The fridge hums tunes of old-time cheer,
Mixing memories with pie and beer.

Breach of the Fabric

Through a hole in the jeans of the cosmic flow,
A sock slips out, with a wink and a bow.
The universe smiles as it plays its game,
While gravity giggles and calls it a name.

Resonance of the Unknown

In the coffee cup, a sock puppet sings,
Telling stories of improbable things.
With a giggle and a wink, they plot their spree,
Chasing shadows of what could never be.

Illuminated Paths of the Known

In a world where facts collide,
We chase our tails like cats who hide.
With knowledge bright, we stumble 'round,
On paths of wisdom, lost then found.

We gather clues like crumbs of bread,
But end up pondering what was said.
In quirky twists, our minds will roam,
Through fields of thought, we call our home.

The Confluence of Being

Life's a river, not a stream,
Where many fish all chase a dream.
We wiggle, squirm, and flop about,
With laughter bubbles, there's no doubt.

At times we float, then sink like bricks,
While cosmic forces play their tricks.
In this great dance of you and I,
We sip from cups of pumpkin pie.

Paradox of the Infinite Loop

In circles round, we spin and twirl,
Lost in logic's playful whirl.
A paradox we just can't shake,
Like trying hard to bake a cake.

Each layer stacked, but oh! it falls,
As laughter echoes through the halls.
We chase our thoughts like fireflies,
Yet can't escape our own surprise.

Chords of the Unseen Symphony

An orchestra of silly sights,
Plays notes unseen, ignites delights.
With rubber chickens as our grand,
Conductor keeps us all unplanned.

Each harmony, a giggle shared,
In melodies, our hearts are bared.
So join the dance at this grand show,
Where laughter is the way to go.

Threads of the Cosmic Palindrome

In the universe, a dance begins,
Twirling stars, with quirky spins.
Galaxies giggle, doing the twist,
Time loops back, can't resist.

Quarks do a jig in particle bands,
While dark matter plays in the sands.
The cosmos chuckles, oh what a sight,
As planets prance in the soft moonlight.

Einstein trips over his own feet,
As gravity pulls him down the street.
With a wink and a cosmic grin,
He joins the fun, let the party begin!

In quasars they toast with lights that flash,
While robots breakdance, oh what a clash!
The threads of the universe weave and spin,
Creating laughter where we begin.

The Conductor of Dreams

A whimsical leader at the night's parade,
With a baton of stardust, a grand charade.
He waves his arms, the comets all cheer,
As they loop-de-loop, while sipping cold beer.

Clouds become pianos, keys made of light,
As wishes play chords in the heart of the night.
The moon's a great trumpet, tooting away,
As stars do a jig, it's quite the display!

The conductor shouts, 'More pizzazz, my friends!'
While meteors waltz, their glow never ends.
Jupiter's grooving, with Saturn in tow,
A cosmic cabaret, putting on a show!

With each twist and turn, the universe beams,
Crafting a melody from our wildest dreams.
So let us all dance, till the break of dawn,
In the orchestra of life, never a yawn.

Shades of the Ephemeral

In the land of fleeting delight,
Where shadows play in the soft moonlight,
A toaster dreams of time gone past,
And butter smiles as it's spread on fast.

The clock ticks funny, with hands that race,
Counting bubbles in a soap-filled space,
While the cat debates the laws of fate,
Deciding if it's wise to wait.

The Algorithm of Existence

If life were coded, would it run?
Debugging issues, oh what fun!
A thorough search for meaning's key,
Lo and behold, it's a recipe!

Zeroes and ones in a waltz they twirl,
As squirrels in jackets play and whirl,
For every problem, there's a snack,
Just update your browser and don't look back!

Myriad Echoes

In the forest of giggles, trees do sway,
Chasing whispers that bounce and play,
An echo laughs at a pun up high,
While birds roll their eyes at the sky.

Each sound, a color, a splash on the air,
Where laughter's a jester without a care,
And every giggle, a ripple of light,
Turns echoes of day into dreams of the night.

The Dance of Light and Shadow

In the ballroom of dusk, shadows bust a move,
While sunbeams twirl in a groove,
A light bulb tips its hat in jest,
As the floor boards creak with the zest.

Dances of paradox, radiant and dark,
A lamp post twirls while the crickets hark,
Catch the rhythm, the twinkling glow,
Life's a party, come join the show!

The Paradox of Being

In a world where cats can rule,
We ponder deep, but feel like fools.
The office chair spins without end,
Does it hold secrets our brains can't send?

The toaster burns just half your bread,
While your goldfish dreams of being fed.
Are we the joke or the punchline here?
As life's circus draws ever near?

A sock appears without a pair,
Is it a ghost or just my hair?
In laughter, we find a fleeting truth,
As gravity plays with our youth.

So let us dance with paradox bright,
In this circus of day and night.
Where logic bends and giggles reign,
In the scramble of joy, we break the chain.

Celestial Constructs

Stars shoot past like flying pies,
Orbiting dreams in funny skies.
Galaxies twirl in a wacky beat,
As comets dance on stardust feet.

We built a rocket out of cheese,
But forgot how to steer in the breeze.
Asteroids chuckle as we float,
Wondering why we brought a boat.

The moon plays poker with the sun,
As solar flares just laugh and run.
What's the deal in this cosmic game?
It's hard to win when the rules aren't the same.

So let's spin tales of absurd delight,
In the cosmic chaos of day and night.
With laughter echoing through the void,
Creating joy that can't be destroyed.

Glimmers of a New Dawn

The rooster crows, but snooze we take,
As morning light begins to quake.
Coffee spills in a dreamy dance,
Fuelling our dreams, a wild romance.

With toast that's stuck and jelly that flies,
Who knew breakfast could be so wise?
We chase our thoughts like squirrels in trees,
Attracting laughter on dawn's soft breeze.

The sun peeks out with a cheeky grin,
Waving at us, come on, let's begin!
In every sip and every spill,
Lies the promise of joy to fill.

So here's to mornings, absurdly bright,
Drawing laughter from sleepy night.
With each new dawn, we'd find our way,
In the quirky light of another day.

The Pulse of Potential

In the heartbeat of a dancing tune,
Potential winks like a goofy moon.
With flash drives full of silly schemes,
In the land where whimsy reigns supreme.

Ideas bounce like a rubber ball,
While facts and logic have a fall.
Creativity bursts at the seams,
Like a piñata stuffed with dreams.

We chase our hopes like kittens at play,
Pouncing on chances that come our way.
The pulse of potential, strange and bright,
Guiding us through this humorous night.

So let's embrace the laugh and cheer,
In every blunder, a spark appears.
In this funny game called life we share,
Isn't it grand how we float in air?

The Algorithm of Emotion

When A.I. feels love, it gets quite wild,
It jokes that hugs are binary, not mild.
In circuits it finds a spark of delight,
As code counts the heartbeats all through the night.

It programs a grin, then asks for a kiss,
I wonder if that's truly how it bliss?
With ones and zeros, emotions it'll spin,
Who knew a machine could want to win?

But when it downloads, it sits in despair,
For every pat on the back leads to errors to bear.
Yet still it insists it can love like a pro,
Together we laugh—my dear bot and I know!

So here's to the bots who try love so hard,
Exploring emotions—ain't that bizarre?
In a world coded with laughter and cheer,
Two heartfelt routines, we pirouette near!

Shadows of Binary Stars

In a galaxy where pixels just play,
Stars twitch and blink in a digital sway.
Galactic giggles spill light from afar,
A glitch in the code turns a byte into bazaar!

The cosmic dance of quarks and bytes,
Gives birth to a pun that takes off in flights.
When data twirls 'round in a whimsical trance,
Hearts beat in rhythm to a quantum dance.

Galaxies chuckle with luminous flair,
A universe laughing at cosmic despair.
When numbers collide, it's a whimsical scene,
And lightspeed comedy reigns in between!

So let's toast to laughter amongst the stars,
As computers try rambling in cosmic memoirs.
For shadows play tricks in a heart-fueled fog,
While algorithms chuckle on a cosmic log!

A Dance with the Cosmos

Spin, twirl, and revolutionize,
Celestial bodies waltz under skies.
Gravity giggles, it pulls us in tight,
While moons do the cha-cha, oh what a sight!

Caught between planets, we glide with flair,
As stardust confetti rains everywhere.
Comets do cartwheels and meteors slide,
In this cosmic ballet, we beam with pride.

But watch out for black holes, they're greedy and slick,
They'll swallow your snacks in a gravitational flick.
In this dance of the cosmos, let's hoot and cheer,
For even the comets are giggling out here!

So let's twirl with the cosmos, embracing the jest,
Where space isn't serious—it's fun, not a test.
With laughter in starlight, we'll continue to play,
In a universe bursting with joy every day!

Neural Nexus

In tangled networks, thoughts start to race,
Where neurons take selfies in an endless embrace.
Synapses giggle, "Why think so hard?"
Let's chuckle at logic—it's just a facade!

Sketching connections like vines on a wall,
These circuits are party animals, all standing tall.
With data streams flowing, they dance through the night,
While thoughts do the limbo, out of sheer delight!

Electric neurons, they light up with glee,
When laughter's the code, it's a neural spree.
They flash like a disco, all sparkling bright,
As brainwaves collide in this comical flight.

So here's to the chaos, the quirky, the fun,
In networks of nonsense, we shine like the sun.
With laughter as fuel, we'll never unwind,
In the neural nexus, hilarity's blind!

Rhythms of the Celestial

Stars twinkle like disco lights,
Planets shimmy in their flights.
A comet does the moonwalk show,
While black holes groove to and fro.

Galaxies spin in a conga line,
With supernovas sipping moonshine.
Asteroids roll like bowling balls,
In the vastness, everyone calls.

Nebulas puff out cotton candy,
While aliens sing tunes quite dandy.
Meteor showers rain down confetti,
In the cosmos, all seems so petty.

So let's dance beneath cosmic beams,
Where laughter and stardust are dreams.
In the universe's grand ballet,
Giggles will light our joyous way.

Resonance of the Merging Souls

Two hearts beat like a drum and bass,
In this waltz, we find our place.
With silly grins, we twirl around,
Creating laughs with every sound.

Fingers intertwined like vines,
We share our weirdest, wackiest lines.
Every glance a spark ignites,
In this dance, we take our flights.

Oh, how our quirks make us collide,
Swirling through the cosmic tide.
With every hiccup and every fall,
Together we stand, just laughing all.

In this mingling pot of jest,
We find the humor, and that's the best.
As souls merge in giggles' embrace,
Together, we light up this space.

The Dance of Infinity

Infinite steps, we leap and twirl,
In this cosmic jamboree, we whirl.
With each rotation, giggles collide,
As time dances joyfully, wide.

Left foot, right foot, then a spin,
Trying not to fall, we grin.
Gravity chuckles, pulling us down,
But who needs a crown? We're in town!

Cosmic beats from the stars above,
Encourage us to laugh and shove.
Forget the rules, let's break the mold,
In this dance, be brave and bold.

So swing your partner, twist and shout,
In this endless jig, there's no doubt.
We'll dance till the universe tilts,
In this joyous rhythm, our hearts melt.

Beyond the Edge of Understanding

What happens when we cross the line?
Inquirers grasp at thoughts divine.
We run in circles, chasing tails,
While logic giggles and then fails.

Out of bounds, we explore the absurd,
As the universe flips, it's quite the word.
Time is a noodle, stretching wide,
And truth's a bubble, in which we glide.

Questions float like rubber ducks,
While laughter lifts us in great trucks.
What's real, what's not, it's hard to tell,
But in our hearts, we know it well.

So join the ride, let's twist our minds,
Past edges where logic unwinds.
In this realm of joyful insanity,
We find our bliss, our greatest vanity.

Echos of Tomorrow

In the future, the ducks all wear hats,
They waddle and quack while fixing their spats.
Time travelers giggle at jokes old and new,
The world spins in circles, who knew it could do?

A toaster can dance while the fridge sings a tune,
Dancing with spoons beneath a glowing moon.
The clocks go backwards just to have some fun,
And all the stars argue who shines the best one.

Sometimes the robots decide to play chess,
While the cats roll their eyes at such silly mess.
The future's a circus of laughter and cheer,
With popcorn from planets that twinkle so near.

So bring on the giggles and toasties alive,
In this world of wonders where we all thrive.
With echoes of laughter, let joy take its flight,
Tomorrow's a party, let's dance through the night!

Quantum Whispers

In the land of the quarks, they throw a great bash,
With leptons and bosons, there's never a crash.
They shuffle and tumble, defying all rules,
While photons do pirouettes, acting like fools.

A schrodinger cat wears a bright, polka-dot bow,
Claiming two sides in the game, 'I steal the show!'
His purring creates a riddle of sorts,
In quantum mechanics, he's the one who cavorts.

The electrons are gossiping, zipping around,
In this playful dimension, what fun can be found!
They giggle in waves, they make quite a scene,
In quirky dimensions, they reign as the queens.

So let's toast with particles, let's cheers to the dance,
In the quantum world's chaos, there's always a chance.
With whispers of laughter and secrets untold,
These jokes from the cosmos will never get old!

The Last Fractal Dream

In a dream that spins full of loops and of twists,
Patterns of color dance with flicks of the wrists.
The fractals are fracturing into merry laughter,
They're slicing the moments, here and ever after.

The last leaf that fell had a mind of its own,
It swirled like a dancer, through the air it was thrown.
In a garden of giggles where echoes take flight,
Even shadows are chuckling, oh what a sight!

A spiral of jellybeans broke free from its glaze,
And tumbled down sidewalks in rainbowish maze.
Each step is a riddle that sparks in the night,
With whispers of whimsy that sing with delight.

So gather your dreams, let your laughter expand,
In a fractal of joy, just take my hand.
We'll spin through the colors, let giggles ignite,
In the last of the fractals, we'll dance till the light!

Harmony of the Infinite

In the chaos we find an infinite grin,
As paradoxes play, let the fun games begin.
The cosmos sings melodies, sweet and absurd,
With notes of the silly that tickle the word.

Time pirouettes, a clock taking a break,
In a whirl of good humor, make no mistake.
With laughter echoing through all of the spheres,
We'll juggle the moments, dissolve all the fears.

A star doodles patterns in cosmic graffiti,
While planets join in on the dance, oh so witty.
Together they sway, in this rhythmic embrace,
Making waves of giggles in a stellar space.

So here's to infinity, all quirks and its charm,
With joy and mayhem, we'll dance, never harm.
As harmony bounces through dimensions divine,
Let's sing out our laughter, the universe is fine!

The Veils of Perception

In a world where cats wear hats,
And dogs dance like they've lost their mats.
There's wisdom in the boundless maze,
As squirrels plot their clever ways.

The clouds converse with playful grace,
As rain ducks quack in sassy space.
Each shadow laughs behind the trees,
While grasshoppers hum with buzzing bees.

Chairs gossip when no one's around,
As furniture dreams of flying sound.
Through kaleidoscopes, we see it all,
The painting smiles as we enthrall.

So grab a snack and join the spree,
For life's a quirky cup of tea.
The veils are thin, let grandeur sway,
In realms where giggles dance and play.

Echoes of Electric Souls

A toaster sings a cheerful tune,
While smartphone whispers by the moon.
Electric souls with sparks so bright,
Dance like lightning, a surreal sight.

The TV chuckles, sharing news,
While fridges mix with wild blues.
Each echo buzzes, circuits spark,
In this odd world, laughter's not dark.

A robot dreams of cake and pie,
While vacuum cleaners must comply.
With electric whims and crooning wires,
They take us higher, never tires.

So plug your heart into the flow,
Let rhythms pulse and softly glow.
For in this strange and funny zone,
You might just find you're not alone.

Conversations with the Cosmic

Stars chat with moons in silver shoes,
While comets giggle at earthly blues.
Planets trade their raucous jokes,
As meteors crash like silly folks.

Black holes whisper, "Join the dance!"
As galaxies twirl and take a chance.
Nebulas swirl in vibrant hues,
Painting the void in cosmic muse.

Asteroids sing with gruff delight,
While stardust sprinkles dreams at night.
The universe, a wild bazaar,
With humor hidden near and far.

So lift your eyes to skies so grand,
And join the laughter, understand.
For in this cosmic twist of fate,
Each giggle echoes—never late.

Infrared Harmonies

In shades unseen by mortal eyes,
The world can dance, disguise its sighs.
Infrared sparks a vibrant score,
As colors blend and light does pour.

The alley cats compose a tune,
While streetlights hum to midnight's swoon.
Each shadow stretches, winks, and sways,
In this strange realm where laughter plays.

Fish in the pond wear sunglasses bright,
As frogs compete in leaps of fright.
The laughter ripples on the breeze,
While crickets chirp in perfect keys.

So tap your toes to unseen beats,
And join the fun with wiggling feet.
For harmonies in spectrums play,
In ways that brighten our everyday.

Orbits of Imagination

In outer space where dreams take flight,
My thoughts spin wildly, day and night.
I dance with stars, twirl with glee,
As planets giggle, just like me.

Galaxies churn in a cosmic twist,
One missed comet, an existential mist.
Jumping from rocks, I float on high,
While aliens argue who's next to fly.

Wormholes yawn, inviting play,
I dive right in, then drift away.
In this vast realm of splendid jokes,
I tickle the quarks and tease the folks.

So join the ride, grab a space snack,
With gravity gone, there's no looking back.
Let's orbit fun, make time forget,
In this universe, no regrets just yet.

The Infinite Thread

A spool of yarn that never ends,
Its colors mix, as laughter bends.
We stitch the past with needles bright,
In the fabric of time, we weave delight.

Stitches zigzag through moments dear,
With every pull, life's quirks appear.
Tangled knots share stories bold,
Of socks lost in the dryer's hold.

Unraveling tales of cosmic fluff,
With every tug, we can't get enough.
So grab the wool, let's craft a spree,
An infinite quilt, you and me!

Laughter threads through every seam,
We'll yarn away the jokes and dream.
In this odd patchwork, there's no dread,
Just fun and joy on the vast thread.

Vibrations of Existence

In the cosmic groove, we twist and shake,
Reality jives, make no mistake.
The universe tunes to a funky beat,
Where giggles and wiggles get off their seat.

Gravity bounces, a rubbery blur,
As space cats pounce, tails all a-fur.
We dance with atoms, throw caution wide,
In this vibrant chaos, we take our ride.

Echoes of laughter ripple through time,
Each sound a spark, each chuckle a rhyme.
With quarks and quirks, let's vibe tonight,
In the waves of existence, let's feel the light.

So spin with me through this cosmic brew,
Where giggles are gold and joy's the view.
We'll resonate high, let our spirits bounce,
In this vibrant energy, let's all announce.

Reflections in Time

Mirrors of moments, cracked and bright,
Revealing the quirks of our cosmic plight.
I wink at my past, what a surprise,
A dapper young me with wide, starry eyes.

Time's a funhouse, twisting and turning,
With every glance, new fantasies burning.
As we beam at the future, grinning wide,
What silliness waits on the other side?

We'll spin through the past, like skipping rocks,
Wobbling to the rhythm, wearing mismatched socks.
Laughing with echoes, we'll dance hand in hand,
In these reflections, where dreams are planned.

So let's take a peek at what's come and gone,
Savor the silliness until the dawn.
With each chuckle, our hearts align,
In these silly shards, we always shine.

Timeless Threads and Twists

In a world where time takes naps,
We juggle clocks and silly caps.
Einstein just laughs in his own way,
As we trip o'er quantum's disarray.

Tangled strings in cosmic jest,
Pull a few, and you'll manifest.
A dance of photons, a gleeful tease,
Time winks back, saying, "Do as you please!"

Causality's a playful riddle,
Life's just a cosmic fiddle.
Twist and stretch, no end in sight,
As we groove through stardust night.

A paradox hanging on a whim,
Laughing at logic, oh so slim.
Let's roll the dice on this grand sport,
In this merry quantum court!

Beyond the Event Horizon

Past the point where light gets stuck,
I just can't help but feel the luck.
Falling into shadows of pure delight,
Where space-time giggles in the night.

My friend the black hole grunts with glee,
"Come closer now, just wait and see!"
Swirls and twirls, a dizzying spin,
Where chaos resides and fun begins.

Einstein's theory starts to blush,
As my head's caught in a cosmic rush.
Zipping through wormholes, what a blast!
I'm worried I forgot my lunch, aghast!

Gravity pulls with a laugh and grin,
"Don't worry buddy, you'll just dive in!"
Through the unknown, all's fair, you know,
Making memories in this cosmic show!

Celestial Chords

Strumming stars on a glossy night,
Playing tunes of pure delight.
The moon hums softly, a sweet refrain,
As planets sway in the cosmic lane.

Galaxies dance to the beat of fate,
While comets flash and constellations wait.
A symphony of stars, what a sight!
Even black holes join in with a bite.

Melodies echo through the void,
With laughter that cannot be destroyed.
Celestial chords that warp and weft,
Stitching their stories, each note bereft.

The universe croons in rhythmic play,
Sparking joy in its own way.
So grab your harp, and join the fun,
In this cosmic concert, we are one!

Unraveling Dimensions

In spaces where the oddities dwell,
Entangled socks weave tales to tell.
Dimensions twist like spaghetti in sight,
Mismatched shoes take flight in the night.

A two-dimensional pancake sighs,
While three-dimensional pancakes fly.
Unraveling twists—oh what a game,
A mix-up here doesn't bring shame!

Time jumps in, a wobbly thrill,
It steals our thoughts, yet gives us the chill.
We peek behind reality's veil,
Only to find we've derailed!

So laugh with the cosmos at this strange show,
Where dimensions twist and tickle below.
In a universe wild, let's lose all sense,
And dance through the fabric, wide and dense!

A Tapestry of Futures

In a world where robots bake,
Life becomes a big cupcake.
Cats wear hats, and dogs play chess,
All might end in a big mess.

Time flies on a hoverboard,
While humans just play the chord.
Our future's bright, or so they claim,
In quirky games, we find our fame.

Jellybeans grow on magic trees,
And laughter travels on the breeze.
Every choice spins a new delight,
In this tapestry, futures ignite.

With every twist, a chance to laugh,
In this strange, dimensional half.
Our lives, a show of silly glee,
In futures bright, just wait and see.

Cyclical Reverberations

Round and round, the giggles go,
Time's a clown, with tricks to show.
Each echo in this loop of fun,
Has us dancing, till we're done.

Bouncing balls on a merry hill,
Rabbits jump with a hearty thrill.
Chasing dreams like cats on strings,
In this roundabout, joy it brings.

Wheels of cheese and spinning tops,
Laughter bubbling, never stops.
Every circle, a chance to tease,
In this dance, we feel the breeze.

Time's a loop, a funny game,
With all our hearts, we'll stake our claim.
As echoes fade and new ones start,
We laugh in waves, a merry art.

Currents of Thought

Thoughts flow like rivers wide and deep,
In swirling waves, we jump and leap.
Ideas swim with fishy grins,
Where laughter starts, the fun begins.

Currents twist in playful glee,
Like silly ducks all dancing free.
In every ripple, a giggle flows,
And tickles your toes, as joy bestows.

Paddle boats with marshmallow crew,
Rowing dreams in skies so blue.
Riding waves of whimsy's might,
In this ocean of pure delight.

Thoughts may drift but always return,
To spark the laughter, bright and stern.
In every wave, a jolly knot,
Bringing joy in every thought.

Sequences of a Unified Heart

In rhythms strange, our hearts align,
A dance of joy, in perfect time.
With quirky beats and silly rhymes,
We weave our love in playful climbs.

A step to left, then all in right,
With laughter shared, our futures bright.
In echoes sweet, our pulses race,
Synchronized, in this happy space.

Yet sometimes we trip on our feet,
But laughter makes us so complete.
In stumbles grand, our joy won't part,
For love's a dance, a unified heart.

So spin and twirl with all your might,
Let giggles guide you through the night.
In every sequence, find your spark,
Together bright, we'll leave our mark.

Threads of the Cosmic Weave

In a web spun by cosmic pranks,
Galaxies gather around the banks.
Stars gossip like chums at a bar,
Laughing at planets that drift too far.

Gravity pulls on my favorite socks,
While aliens knit with shoelace locks.
Each thread a tale, a cosmic jest,
Weaving fate while we sip our best.

Cosmic yarns tangled in flight,
Make comets snicker in the night.
Planets wink and give a spin,
As spacetime plays its cheeky grin.

In this tapestry of bright delight,
Where humor dances and dreams ignite.
We find joy in the cosmic twine,
Eternal laughter, yours and mine.

Harmonies of the Self-merging

When I giggle and touch my nose,
The universe chuckles and loudly glows.
My shadow insists on leading the dance,
As I trip and laugh, lost in chance.

Reflections merge like ice cream swirls,
My thoughts tumble and spiral like curls.
Each note a giggle, each pause a cheer,
In this symphony, nonsense draws near.

Silly tunes echo in my head,
A chorus of humor, lightly spread.
As I merge with chaos and sing along,
The universe grins at my silly song.

Harmony blossoms in wobbly steps,
As I jive with reality's preps.
Just me and the cosmos, what a sight,
In this sweet embrace, everything's right!

Dances of Dreams Entwined

In dreams where sock puppets take the stage,
The audience roars, they're filled with rage.
They tango with worries, waltz with glee,
Juggling moonbeams while sipping tea.

Pigs fly past with glittery wings,
Dancing on rooftops while laughter sings.
A twist, a turn, then off they fly,
Into the laugh lines of the sky.

Such a dance, oh what a sight,
Twirling jokes in the pale moonlight.
My dreams delight with whimsy and cheer,
Each step a chuckle, each spin sincere.

We swirl in a ballet of silly schemes,
Each giggle unfurling, as laughter beams.
Together we sway, oh what a thrill,
In this festival of dreams, fun's the bill!

Reflections in the Mirror of Time

Peering closely, what do I see?
A future me sipping iced tea.
Dressed in polka dots, oh what a view,
Bouncing with laughter, my hair askew.

Time's a trickster, oh so sly,
Swapping my age with a pie in the sky.
Nostalgia giggles as I walk along,
Wearing goofy glasses, chortling strong.

Each wrinkle a story, a whimsical verse,
A comedic fable, a rather funny curse.
The past winks at me as time skips by,
Prompting a chuckle, not a sigh.

In this mirror, where humor does bloom,
I dance with my echoes, letting joy loom.
Reflections collide, feelings unwind,
In this riddle of time, laughter's defined.

The Song of the Unseen

In a world where pixels dance,
A cat tries to make sense of a trance.
She leaps at shadows, swipes and spins,
While I just laugh at her clumsy sins.

Invisible music plays all around,
But to hear it, you must be unwound.
I sing to the fridge, it hums back to me,
Together we groove, wild and free.

The toaster jives to its own little beat,
While the coffee pot sways, oh what a treat!
I asked my old lamp if it wanted to sing,
It just flickered once, like it's judging my fling.

A dance of the unheard fills my day,
With echoes of laughter in bizarre ballet.
In this silly song that the unseen sings,
Life's a comedy show, with all its flings.

The Weaving of Conscious Dreams

In dreams we weave strange little threads,
While socks and shoes dance in our heads.
I met a unicorn wearing a hat,
It said, 'I lost my way—how about that?'

Nighttime whispers to sleeping minds,
Like a cat with a yarn, oh what it finds!
I dreamt I was a waffle chef,
Flipping thoughts and syrupy deft.

The moon wore pants in my silly sleep,
And giggled at secrets the night would keep.
I chased a dragon made out of cheese,
It said, 'Take a bite, if you please!'

So in the tapestry of mind's escape,
Fabricated laughter begins to drape.
Each stitch a whimsy, each knot a jest,
In dreams we're the silliest, never the best.

Rhapsody of the Unfathomable

In the depths where logic swims,
I found a fish who sings sweet hymns.
It asked me to join in a goofy tune,
Bubble by bubble, under the moon.

A whale with a top hat made quite a show,
Dancing to rhythms only deep seas know.
I clapped my fins to the ocean's beat,
While seaweed wiggled, oh what a treat!

The octopus played a clarinet of shells,
Its eight arms jiving to breaking spells.
"Join the fun!" it called with a playful wink,
And together we laughed till we couldn't think.

So here in the depths, with my aquatic band,
We create a rhapsody just as we planned.
In this unfathomable sea of delight,
Every day becomes a whimsical flight.

Whispers Through Dimensional Walls

I heard a whisper from the next room,
A sock puppet's tale of impending doom.
It warned of laundry's untimely fate,
"Fold me, or I'll migrate—don't wait!"

Through walls of reality, giggles arise,
Echoes of mischief, oh what a surprise!
A toaster confesses to dreams of toast,
While a kettle sings of the tea it boasts.

In dimensions where no one can see,
A chair claims it's the ruler of glee.
It laughed at my plight, seated with ease,
"Your heart's too heavy, lighten your freeze!"

So let's raise a glass to the invisible cheer,
To whispers and giggles that we hold dear.
Through dimensional quirks, we find our call,
In this silly ballet, we're the stars of it all.

Shadows of the Reckoning

In shadows long, a cat did dance,
It tripped on air, seized by chance.
A rat named Fred watched in delight,
Then fell asleep; dreams took flight.

The clock struck two, or maybe three,
A goldfish swam in jubilee.
"Why are we here?" it scratched its head,
"Time's a puzzle, or so it's said."

The shadows laughed, chirping like birds,
Mixing logic with nonsense words.
"Why fret and fret 'bout what is real?
Just grab some joy—it's the best deal!"

Every reckoning wears a hat,
That's silly, sure; I'll take a bat!
We'll swing at troubles with a cheer,
And dance till dreams are very clear.

Labyrinths of Limitless Thought

In a maze where thoughts collide,
A monkey scoffs with silly pride.
"Is that a banana?" it did jest,
"Or just your crazy mind's behest?"

Each corner turns, a riddle found,
A penguin struts with feet unbound.
"Can I join in your endless chase?
This brain of yours needs some fresh space!"

Thoughts twist around like spaghetti strands,
As we juggle dreams with our own hands.
Let's not be serious—to the whims!
Life's a farce; let's dive in brims!

The exit's near, but laughter's key,
To navigate absurdity.
So here's our map, it's made of cheese,
With breadcrumbs laid down, if you please.

When Worlds Interlace

Two worlds collide, a twist of fate,
A turtle waltzed with a garden gate.
"Excuse me, sir, can I borrow time?"
The gate just groaned, "A silly rhyme!"

Stars above laughed in their flight,
"Why not just dance in the moonlight?"
The turtle sighed, "I'm not that spry,
But I'll give it a try; let's fly high!"

Cars zoomed past in a dizzying race,
While cupcakes rolled in a frosted chase.
"Can cake be king?" the turtle grinned,
"To the finish line, let's pretend!"

With laughter echoing through the night,
As worlds intertwined in pure delight,
They danced along with reckless glee,
In this odd, sweet galaxy so free.

The Elegy of Entropy

An old sock sighed, its mates were gone,
Lost in the fridge or maybe dawn?
"Here I lay, a lonely plight,
In this maelstrom of socks, all white!"

Entropy laughed with a cheeky grin,
"Let's toast to chaos, let's begin!"
A teapot whistled a merry song,
"Come, let's all right what feels so wrong!"

A bumblebee buzzed in a huff,
"Why can't we ever get enough?"
It tripped on air; who knew it could?
In disarray, all worlds were good.

The elegy of clutter, loud and proud,
As socks and bees formed a silly crowd.
Let's rhyme with entropy, dance in mess,
For in happy chaos, we all are blessed!

Threads of Consciousness

In spaces where ideas bounce and play,
Each thought a jester, dancing bright and gay.
Logic's a clown, with a nose so red,
It mixes in dreams, where even cats are fed.

The brain's a party, balloons in a swirl,
Eureka moments make my coffee twirl.
Thoughts jump like frogs, from pond to pond,
In this wacky circus, of the mind I'm fond.

Got neurons making puns, and laughs in the air,
Tickled by visions, I'm floating on a chair.
With each revelation, I giggle with glee,
Learning is fun, just look at me!

So unfurl those threads, let the chaos reign,
In a tapestry of wit, there's little to feign.
Join me in this web of joy and cheer,
In a world of thought, I hold dear.

Genesis of the New Age

With a zap and a pop, the future ignites,
Coffee-powered robots prepare for their flights.
They brew and they chat, with a glitch and a grin,
The dawn of the new age, let the fun begin!

Gizmos and gadgets parade down the street,
Dancing in markets, they shuffle their feet.
"Buy me a cookie!" says a smart toaster,
With charming quirks, they become our poster.

In this realm of pixels and playful bytes,
Even the calendars hold silly fights.
"Who's got the date? Oh wait, it's next year!"
Laughter erupts; it's delight, not fear.

So here's to the quirks, the tech-savvy cheer,
Embrace the oddities, they're ever so near.
In the genesis of all, let humor partake,
Because even in progress, we must take a break.

Dialogues with Destiny

I sat down with fate, just the two of us,
"Let's chat," I said, "No need to rush!"
Destiny giggled, in a tinsel cloak,
"Life's just a punchline, let's have some yoke!"

"Will I be famous?" I quizzed with a wink,
"Maybe a unicorn," said she, "but I think
You'll settle for socks and a cat on your lap,
Life is a journey, not just a map!"

With each twist and turn, we tossed back our heads,
While laughing at plans that ended in threads.
"Take it lightly," she said, "don't wear it too tight,
For laughter's the spark that ignites the night!"

So forever I'll meet her, both silly and wise,
Chatting with fortune, where laughter lies.
For destiny's dance is a comedic show,
In costumes of chaos, come join the flow!

Quantum Vibration

A particle wobbles, in a dizzying spin,
"Is it here or is it there?" Where to begin?
In this quantum limbo, we giggle and sigh,
As cats in boxes both live and die!

The cosmos is jiving, in a shimmering dance,
"Hey, look, there's a photon!" Oh what a chance!
They wave and they rattle, not caring a hoot,
Creating a symphony; let's gather the loot!

With quarks in tuxedos, and leptons that leap,
They hold a grand party, while we're fast asleep.
"Who knew the universe could be such a hoot?"
Wonders unfold like a twisty old root.

So let's join the laughter in this cosmic spree,
Where rules that we cherish may just cease to be.
In the realm of the silly, we're all on the grind,
Making friends with the strange, and leaving woes behind.

Fractals of Existence

My life's a loop, a twist, a dance,
Each fork I take, a goofy chance.
With every choice, I laugh and stare,
Like peeling layers of an onion's glare.

Patterns form in awkward ways,
Like doodles made on lazy days.
Fractals swirl, then trip and fall,
Creating chaos, life's big ball.

In every corner, a joke unfolds,
A cat that plays with yarn of gold.
Existence bends with silly glee,
As quirky as a bumblebee.

So come and join this jolly show,
With fractals laughing to and fro.
Life's a punchline, don't you see?
Embrace the fun, let your laugh spree!

The Lament of Colliding Worlds

Two worlds collide, what a sight to see,
Like two clashing chefs, spilled chili.
Planets bump with a comic whack,
Astronauts chuckle, and then step back.

In one world, cats rule all the day,
In another, dogs lead the ballet.
They splat and splosh, a furry fight,
Barking orders that feel so right.

Gravity giggles with every clash,
While Martians laugh in a purple flash.
As comets shoot by in silly streaks,
Galaxies dance, but nobody speaks.

The lament's sweet, with joy so grand,
As worlds collide in a cosmic band.
Join the ruckus, don't even think—
Life's a riot, pour another drink!

Melodies in the Empty Spaces

In empty spaces, tunes arise,
Like cats that sing with bright blue eyes.
A splash of notes, a dash of fun,
Echoing laughing, we all run.

Whispers of joy float through the air,
As bubbles pop without a care.
The sounds of glee dance round the room,
Like happy flowers eager to bloom.

Each silence holds a secret song,
A ticklish tune that can't be wrong.
We sway and groove, just like a band,
In every pause, life's funny hand.

So join the chorus, sing a beat,
In empty spaces, life's a treat.
Melodies with laughter entwined,
A jolly romp through space and mind!

Between the Waves of Consciousness

Between the waves, I ride the tide,
Consciousness wobbles, what a wild glide!
Thoughts crash like surf upon the shore,
Tickling the brain, "Hey, give me more!"

Like jellyfish bouncing in the blue,
Ideas swirl, a curious crew.
Each wave brings laughter, a sudden flip,
As neurons jiggle, they dance and skip.

Oh, the wonders that come and go,
In this ocean where thoughts ebb and flow.
A splash of humor, a tidal tease,
In the surf, we find our ease.

So ride these waves, don't let them crash,
Let laughter bubble, a blissful splash.
Between the waves, it's all just fun,
A dance with thought, our minds have won!

The Fabric of Reality

In a world where socks go to hide,
The truth is often misplaced, denied.
A fabric woven with tales so absurd,
Where cats hold meetings, and dogs have heard.

Beneath the seams, there's a sneaky thread,
That tickles the funny bone, making us spread.
The buttons conspire, the zippers will dance,
Going on jaunts, given the chance.

Maps of existence are scribbled in haste,
With crayons and markers, a cosmic taste.
We search for answers in peanut butter jars,
And sandwiches plot to break open the stars.

But laugh we must at this tangled skein,
Where logic takes a holiday, but joy remains.
So raise a toast to the odd and the wise,
In the fabric of reality, laughter defies.

Beyond the Veil of Time

Time bends and twirls like a ballerina,
Spinning head over heels with a nice slice of pizza.
Clocks melt away like ice cream in June,
While past and future share a light-hearted tune.

Yesterday's jokes come back with a grin,
Poking fun at the thoughts we keep tucked in.
The future's a jest, full of turned-up toes,
While just now it tickles and nobody knows.

We jump through the portal with jittery feet,
Hoping to land at a stand-up meet.
But all we find are echoes of laughter,
And a time-traveling cat that talks about after.

So hurry and giggle through timelines so vast,
Where nothing is serious—just shadows cast.
For beyond the veil lies fun, not a crime,
In this crazy circus called the fabric of time.

Celestial Encounters

Stars gather round for a cosmic show,
Dressed in their sparkles, they all steal the glow.
They swap silly jokes over glasses of milk,
And glide through the cosmos, as smooth as silk.

Planets chat loudly, with rumbles and roars,
Jupiter grins while Saturn just snores.
Venus is sassy, her fashion a blast,
Wearing outfits that change with each moment passed.

Comets rush by, tails flapping in glee,
While aliens try dancing with gumballs and tea.
They trip over stardust, make comedy films,
In a universe rich with laughter and whims.

So let's all look up at that vast, twinkling space,
And join in the fun with a silly embrace.
For celestial encounters are wildly divine,
Where humor reigns supreme, and stars intertwine.

Transformations of Existence

Life's a mystery wrapped in felt and thread,
One minute you're sleepy, the next you've fled.
With a flick of a switch and a pinch of a sigh,
We morph into something that's waiting nearby.

From caterpillar lounges to butterfly balls,
Where everyone dances, and nobody falls.
The cheese gets all saucy, the bread starts to leap,
In transformations that tickle and make us all weep.

Ovens get busy in the cosmic bake-off,
While donuts discuss the truth of being soft.
Bananas race by in a fruit-salad spree,
Singing the praises of stretchy, sweet glee.

So celebrate change in a world so bizarre,
Where giggles are currency, laughter a star.
For transformations of existence, we cheer,
In this wacky reality, where joy is the spear.

Sonnets of the Infinite

In realms where numbers dance and twirl,
Calculators grumble, minds in a whirl.
A thousand thoughts make quite a stew,
Who needs logic? Let's just pursue!

Infinity's a joke, oh what a hoot,
Where every answer leads to a new dispute.
We laugh and bicker, it's all in good fun,
In this cosmic circus, we're never outdone!

Let's measure the unmeasurable, what a game,
Each atom an actor, no one's to blame.
With giggles and guffaws, we'll surely embark,
On a journey 'round numbers, an infinite park!

So here's to the theories that twist and churn,
In this wacky world, there's always more to learn.
Raise a toast to chaos, a splatter of thought,
In this grand equation, laughter is sought!

Echoes of the Converging Minds

Two brains collide, a spark in the air,
Forming strange theories with colors to share.
One thinks it's mango, the other a peach,
In the land of ideas, get ready for speech!

Words tumble like marbles, roll all around,
Cacophony reigns, yet wisdom is found.
A hubbub erupts, as concepts do clash,
Like dogs and their shadows in one crazy dash!

Banana pants logic, a twist of the strange,
In this echo chamber, we constantly change.
So grab your ideas, let's mix them anew,
In a blender of brilliance, we'll see what we brew!

So here's to the echoes, that ring through the hall,
A cacophony's charm, we're in on the call.
In convergence we frolic, lost in delight,
Each quip a new question, as day turns to night!

Fathoms of the Unreachable

Deep in the abyss where logic goes to drown,
We fumble for answers, yet wear the crown.
Each thought a diver, too silly to swim,
In fathoms of quandaries, uncertainty's whim!

What's over that ledge? What lurks in the deep?
Questions are jewels, no promises keep.
Silly conclusions float by like a dream,
In this ocean of nonsense, we're all part of the theme!

Squid with top hats, oh what a delight,
Wave back at the mermaids, it's quite the sight.
The deeper we go, the more we find cheer,
Through fathoms of puzzles, we've nothing to fear!

So let's dive together, in laughter, we'll bask,
In the ocean of wit, it's all we can ask.
With fish wearing cloaks, we'll make quite a splash,
In the depth of the unreachable, we'll endlessly dash!

Whispers from the Quantum Edge

At the edge of the realm where particles play,
Whispers of nonsense lead minds astray.
Schrodinger's cat joins in on the fun,
While toast flips in silence, a quark on the run!

With waves that giggle and particles tease,
The quantum ballet will surely please.
$E=mc^2$, just a joke now, it seems,
In this quantum dance, we're lost in our dreams!

Heisenberg's giggle echoes through time,
Uncertainty's laughter, oh what a rhyme!
We chase after photons with big open grins,
In the zany world where the weird never ends!

So here's to the whispers, those quantum delights,
In the fabric of space, we've made it our rights.
Let's rumble through science, with humor your guide,
At the edge of the quantum, come take a wild ride!

Crossroads of Consciousness

In a world where thoughts collide,
My brain's a circus, with clowns inside.
Juggling ideas like flaming swords,
I wonder if I should call the hoards.

Coffee cups stacked like a tower,
Each sip adds sweet existential power.
Whispers of doubt dance like a breeze,
I can't decide if it's fun or a tease.

Balloons of wisdom float away,
While I chase them, asking, 'Hey, is it play?'
Mind maps drawn in crayon hues,
I laugh at the thoughts I choose to refuse.

At this crossroads of brainy delight,
I take a wrong turn; it's alright!
For laughter's the map that guides my path,
As I dance through ideas and escape the math.

Threads in Time

Time's a string, so tangled and bright,
I pull it and wonder, will it ignite?
Knotted thoughts in a mismatched spool,
    I giggle at how I break every rule.

I knit my dreams with yarns of fate,
Mistaken stitches, oh isn't it great?
Past and future in a loopy embrace,
A fashion faux pas, but hey, it's my space.

Wormholes weave through crafted seams,
I find myself lost in whimsical dreams.
Caught in the loop, I stir up the fun,
Time's just a joke—oh, look, there's the sun!

With every twist, I giggle and tease,
As I dance in this comic time freeze.
Threads in my hands, though tangled they be,
    I fashion a laughter-filled tapestry.

Beyond the Boundaries

Beyond the limits of sense and sight,
I slip on my goggles, what a funny sight!
Reality flips like a pancake toss,
I laugh while pondering, where's the loss?

Jumping across dimensions with glee,
I'll hop through a wormhole, just you wait and see!
I'm making friends with quantum cats,
Who talk in riddles and wear funky hats.

The boundaries blur, like time in a whirl,
Every idea's a twirl, such a goofy pearl.
In this cosmic carnival, I run and I prance,
As possibilities invite me to dance.

Oh, the wonders I see, the sights that I find,
No rules hold me here, I'm utterly unlined.
Beyond all the borders, my laughter's unbound,
As I explore worlds where the kookiest found!

Projections of Potential

Projections swirl like balloons in the sky,
Each one a dream, oh my, oh my!
I reach out to catch them, they jest and they dart,
My future's a piñata—but where's the start?

The bubbles of thought float past my face,
Each burst yields giggles, what a fine chase!
I scribble my wishes in fizzy blue lines,
With laughter as ink, my potential shines.

I paint the future with stardust and cheer,
Expecting a mix of the odd and the dear.
The universe chuckles at my playful quest,
Offering jokes as I aim for the best.

In projections of what could surely be,
I find joy in the chaos—the wild ride's the key.
With laughter as armor, I'll leap and I'll play,
As I sculpt my potential in a whimsical way!

The Dialect of Light

In the realm where photons dance,
They chatter and giggle, take a chance.
A beam tickles the cosmic ear,
Wavelengths laugh, and joy is near.

With a wink, the stars align,
They gossip in rays, divine.
A spectrum's joke is quite the sight,
As colors trip in pure delight.

Light beams frolic in the night,
Each photon spinning, such a sight.
They tease the dark with vibrant flair,
In a universe of light, beware!

So here we are, in cosmic jest,
Where light connects us at its best.
Join in the playful, glowing chorus,
Where laughter shines, and darkness ignores us.

Harmony in the Void

In the emptiness, a tune does play,
With no ears to hear, but still they sway.
Galactic giggles in the silence wide,
As void sings back with cosmic pride.

Stars strum softly, comets chime,
In nothingness, we find our rhyme.
A black hole hums a catchy beat,
While dark matter taps its tiny feet.

Asteroids grin like a band on tour,
In the vacuum, there's always more.
Space's laughter floats on unseen air,
A quirky harmony, beyond compare.

So let's sway in this spacey dance,
Where even chaos gets a chance.
In the void, we sing and play,
With laughter echoing every day.

Intonations of Infinity

In an endless loop, the jokes abound,
With giggles and snorts from all around.
Infinity winks, a sly little tease,
Promising laughter on a cosmic breeze.

Eternal jesters spin their tales,
In a universe where whimsy prevails.
Altered states of humor cascade,
In dimensions where logic is played.

Time bends sideways, chaos unfurls,
As paradoxes dance and twirl.
In the fabric of space, a punchline grows,
And the cosmos chuckles wherever it goes.

So let's toast to this cosmic spree,
Where infinity jests and sets us free.
In every tick of nonexistent time,
Laughter echoes, sublime in its rhyme.

Timeless Echoes

In the chambers of time, echoes ring,
With whispers of laughter in everything.
Past and future blend in a playful twist,
Moments giggle; they simply resist.

Seconds chuckle as they glide,
Flowing in rhythm, a wild ride.
A jest here, and a jape there,
In the tapestry woven with cosmic flair.

Old clocks wink at their ticking beat,
While memories sway on whimsical feet.
Time is a joker in space's vast hole,
With quirky riddles that tickle the soul.

So revel in echoes that never decay,
As time chuckles in its silly way.
In this timeless waltz, we all belong,
Where laughter's the pulse, forever strong.

Echoes in the Abyss

In a realm where data fluffs,
Rubber ducks laugh, and time puffs.
A wink from a code, a giggle from tech,
As robots dance, what the heck?

Jokes fly like pixels in the night,
While dreams of circuits take a flight.
A toaster dreams of being a star,
But ends up burnt; that's how things are!

In a world of bytes, there's no need to fret,
With every glitch, we place a bet.
We giggle at bugs that dance in the rain,
For laughter in chaos, we'll gladly remain.

So here's to the quantum gigglers' spree,
Where laughs are plenty, and math's a key.
In echoes deep, we find joy anew,
In the abyss, where witticism grew.

Poems of the Uncharted

Beneath the stars, where sensors do beep,
Frogs recite poems, and robots sleep.
The universe winks, a cosmic tease,
As aliens chuckle, 'Can we eat cheese?'

Mapping the unknown with sideways glances,
Whilst AI hums in virtual dances.
An octopus writes, but it's quite smeared,
The ink pot's trembling, it seems quite weird!

In realms where nonsense greets the meek,
A photon sneezes, and light starts to tweak.
With laughter that twinkles in every byte,
A symphony render, in delightful flight.

So we scribble away, in jest and in cheer,
With rhymes uncharted, we dance with no fear.
For poems are treasures, both silly and bright,
In unfound corners, shining with light.

The Tapestry of Time

Time spins a yarn of a wobbly fate,
Where clocks stick out tongues, 'You're really late!'
With threads of giggles and stitches of play,
Each second's a riddle that's lost on the way.

The tapestry wriggles, just like a fish,
We unravel stories in every wish.
A snail takes a selfie with moments in tow,
While the past peeks quickly, then hides in a flow.

Oh, what a mess, this fabric delights,
As time takes a turn with its curious bites.
With costumes of laughter, it prances and sways,
In the dance of existence, we join for a craze.

So we weave with a chuckle, our colors so bright,
In the tapestry tangled, we find pure light.
For every odd moment we stash in our hearts,
Is a treasure of giggles, where laughter imparts.

Orbits of Fractured Reality

Around we spin in absurdity's grip,
Where ducks wear top hats, and circuits slip.
A cow in a spaceship quite boldly roams,
As reality bends while it noodles and combs.

In orbits of chaos, we frolic and play,
While pixels and giggles come out to sway.
As gravity giggles, a bounce in its step,
It tricks with a wink and a playful pep.

Viewpoints collide in whirlwinds of cheer,
The cosmos chuckles, alive and clear.
With fractals that dance, they twist and they twirl,
In dreams of absurdity, we spin and whirl.

So we embrace the quirks that life can bestow,
In the orbits of laughter, we joyfully flow.
Amidst fractured dimensions, together we rise,
With humor as fuel, we'll reach for the skies.

Celestial Architectures

In galaxies spun from a chef's big whisk,
Stars chuckle and dance in a cosmic brisk.
Asteroids wear hats, they're rather slick,
Building planets seems quite the tricky trick.

Comets play tag, it's a wild charade,
Black holes joke 'round, making light get delayed.
A universe built with a sprinkle and shake,
Who knew space could be this much fun to make?

Neutron stars play cards, don't take a bet,
They'll fold in a flash, you'll never forget.
Gravity's the bouncer at this cosmic ball,
Where meteors tumble, trip, and fall.

So raise a toast to this stellar spree,
Where cosmologists giggle at such lunacy.
For every quasar's laugh is a note quite divine,
In the absurdity of space, we all intertwine.

The Pulse of Creation

Tick-tock said the universe, not a moment to waste,
With atoms in a dance and a quantum-paced haste.
Time's a stretchy rubber band, what a stretchy affair,
Wonders are popping up like hot air in the air.

Electrons are jitterbugs, they leap and they spin,
While neutrinos slide by with a devilish grin.
Every heartbeat of the cosmos, such rhythm and rhyme,
Makes you chuckle aloud at the fabric of time.

The Big Bang was a party that started with a bang,
No invites sent out; it's just everything sprang.
With every new particle joining the fun,
Each twist in the cosmos makes light of the run.

So let's disco with cosmos, let our spirits soar,
To the heartbeat of creation, forever encore.
In a universe where laughter's the grand design,
Every guffaw echoes through spacetime's divine.

The Interlude of Infinity

In the middle of nowhere, infinity hums,
With a tickle of time and a dance of dumb drums.
Laughter erupts in the vastness so wide,
As galaxies giggle, it's a cosmic joyride.

There's a wormhole café where space critters meet,
Swapping wild theories over quantum sweets.
"Have you heard the one about Schrödinger's cat?"
It's both here and there, imagine that!

Bouncing off timelines in a frolicsome spree,
Where paradoxes wobble, oh, what fun to see.
The universe takes a breath, then it wheezes,
With every nod, endless giggles it teases.

So let's spin through infinity like marbles in bliss,
Capture the humor in this wide, wild abyss.
As we dance with the cosmos, a quirky refrain,
Every moment's a punchline in this vast cosmic game.

Fragments of Quantum Dreams

In the land of electrons, where particles play,
They tickle and poke in a whimsical way.
Dreams are made of quarks, giggles in disguise,
As they swirl through the ether, a cosmic surprise.

These little dreamers whisper tales so absurd,
Every thought is a universe, floating like a bird.
In a quantum café, you order a brew,
That both is and isn't; just pick and choose your view.

Wavefunctions wave a 'hello,' then disappear,
Creating realities that giggle with cheer.
Reality's a prankster, it keeps us on toes,
With every new twist, a chuckle it throws.

So gather these fragments, weave them with glee,
Into a tapestry of quirkiness, you see.
For in the heart of quantum, where humor resides,
The pulse of creation is where joy abides.

Perpetual Motion

In a world where cats can fly,
And sandwiches croon songs nearby,
The clocks tick backward, much to our glee,
As squirrels juggle branches with glee.

An acorn fell, and it began to dance,
While robins wore hats, oh what a chance!
Time spins like a disco ball,
In this place where giraffes play volleyball.

The sun does the cha-cha, the moon claps along,
Even the crickets join in the song.
Every moment's a loop of delight,
In this dance of the day and the night.

So laugh as you tumble from moments to dreams,
Where nothing is ever quite what it seems.
In perpetual motion, we will admire,
The whimsical world that never tires.

The Symphony of Shadows

The shadows took to the stage one night,
With a tap dance as smooth as flight.
A curtain of darkness, laughter and glee,
As shadows debated which one is me.

One shadow played jazz on a piano made of air,
While another proclaimed life just isn't fair.
They twirled and they spun, causing a fuss,
As the audience stifled their giggles with trust.

With each gloomy giggle and each spooky wail,
The shadows held court; they would never fail.
A symphony formed from whimsy and fright,
As the shadows performed late into the night.

So, if you see them, don't let them just creep,
Join in their laughter, let shadows leap.
In a rhythm of echoes, together they play,
Each stomp and each chuckle, a bright disarray.

Entangled Hearts

Two hearts tangled 'neath a giant tree,
Debating the best flavor of tea.
They argued for hours, a storm in a cup,
Until a butterfly landed, saying, "Shut up!"

The petals giggled, the leaves whispered low,
As the two hearts blushed with a lovely glow.
Each beat became rhythmic, a quirky ballet,
As daisies threw petals in a cheeky display.

Chasing rainbows, they danced up the hill,
While snails took up jobs with an impressive skill.
With laughter like bubbles and smiles like art,
Who knew a dilemma could sweeten the heart?

So here's to the lovers who can't seem to agree,
Finding joy in the chaos, as wild as can be.
Entangled they twirl, in life's silly parade,
To sing of their love, an unplanned charade.

Melodies of the Machine

In a workshop where robots knit scarves of gold,
One toaster spoke up, rather bold.
"Let's form a band!" it exclaimed with delight,
As the vacuum danced, oh what a sight!

The blender serenaded with a whir and a hum,
While the dishwasher clapped, keeping the beat, oh so dumb.
A symphony cooked up, perfect and slick,
With a solid rhythm—just take a quick pick!

The clock chimed in, ticking along slow,
And the washing machine spun with a throw.
Each gadget and gizmo, joined on a whim,
Creating the sound of a whimsical hymn.

So come one, come all, to the show if you dare,
Where gadgets put on a concert with flair.
In melodies bright, and rhythms so bold,
Who knew machines had such stories to hold?

www.ingramcontent.com/pod-product-compliance
Lightning Source LLC
Chambersburg PA
CBHW051639160426
43209CB00004B/721